The Honey Tree

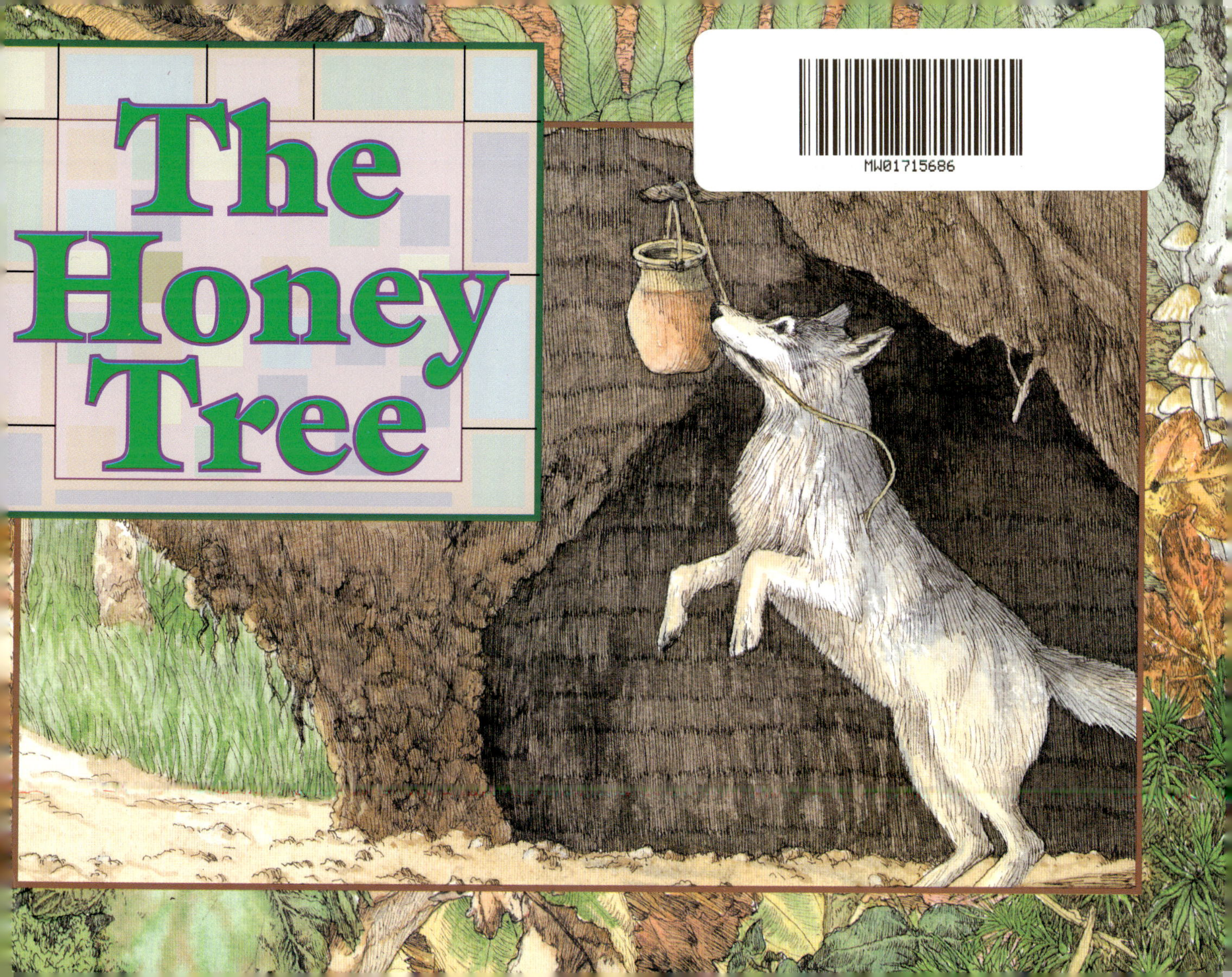

Wolf knew all about honey.
But he kept the secret to himself.

He shared the honey
with his children, who walked
around day and night
with sticky, sweet honey
smeared all over their faces.

Since nobody else knew for sure
where the honey came from,
it was easy for Wolf to trick them.

"Here, this is where honey comes from,"
Wolf said, handing the forest animals
some peaches to eat.

Tortoise didn't trust Wolf.
He wanted to learn
the truth about honey.
He shined up his shell
and went to Wolf's den.

"I would like some honey, please,"
Tortoise said to Wolf.

Wolf tried to trick Tortoise
with a tangerine.
But Tortoise was not so dull.

"I said, I would like
some honey, please,"
Tortoise repeated firmly.

“All right, then,” said Wolf.
“The honey’s in that pot up there.”

Tortoise eyed the pot suspiciously.

“If you lie on your back, you can tip the pot with your toe and the honey will drip out,” said Wolf.

So Tortoise lay down and gave it a try.
What a delight!
He was completely enchanted with the delicious taste of the honey.

But Wolf had a plan to keep his secret.

Tortoise was so absorbed in his feasting that he didn't notice the wolf children bringing in kindling for a fire.

"We'll have roast tortoise for dinner tonight," Wolf said to his children, as they placed the kindling around Tortoise.

Wolf lit the fire and he and the children ran out of the den.

The golden flames licked Tortoise, and Tortoise licked the golden honey.

He didn't even notice the fire. He just went on eating calmly.

It was only when Tortoise had finished all the honey that he rolled over in the ashes, and walked out of the den.

Wolf was amazed to see Tortoise safe and sound.

"You really ought to share the honey with the other animals," Tortoise said.

He winked at Wolf, and Wolf ran off with his tail between his legs.

Tortoise went to
the other forest animals.

"Wolf's been tricking us," he said.
"I've tasted real honey and it's
wonderful."

The animals decided that they would
force Wolf to share the honey.

"We'll give him a taste of his own
medicine," the forest animals said.
"We'll light a fire and smoke him out."

But Wolf didn't come out. Just when the animals were afraid that they had killed Wolf by mistake, a yellow and black bee came swerving out of the cave.

"It's that tricky Wolf, turned into a bee!" Tortoise said. "Let's follow him and find out where he gets his honey."

The animals ran after the bee. The chase took them deep into the forest. Every time the animals thought that they had the bee cornered, it darted off again.

Just when they were about to call off the chase, they caught sight of the bee flying into the hollow of a tree.

"There he goes! **That's** where honey grows!" shouted Tortoise.

He stuck his head into the hollow tree, but pulled it right back out again. A swarm of angry bees appeared at the entrance to the honey tree.

The birds tried to sneak by the bees, but the bees stung them.

Finally a tiny hummingbird darted between the bees. He disappeared for a moment, then emerged with the honey in his beak!

He hovered over the other forest animals, releasing little drops of honey into their mouths.